The No. 1 Way To Prospect

Master The Art of Effortlessly Closing a Potential Client for Business or Sales

JONATHAN S. WALKER

Copyright © 2017 Jonathan S. Walker

All rights reserved.

DEDICATION

I dedicate this book to my two beautiful children and my loving wife who have been nothing short of being my light and joy throughout the years.

Copyright 2017 by Jonathan S. Walker - All rights reserved.

The following eBook is reproduced below with the goal of providing information that is as accurate and reliable as possible. Regardless, purchasing this eBook can be seen as consent to the fact that both the publisher and the author of this book are in no way experts on the topics discussed within and that any recommendations or suggestions that are made herein are for entertainment purposes only. Professionals should be consulted as needed prior to undertaking any of the action endorsed herein.

This declaration is deemed fair and valid by both the American Bar Association and the Committee of Publishers Association and is legally binding throughout the United States.

Furthermore, the transmission, duplication or reproduction of any of the following work including specific information will be considered an illegal act irrespective of if it is done electronically or in print. This extends to creating a secondary or tertiary copy of the work or a recorded copy and is only allowed with express written consent from the Publisher. All additional right reserved.

The information in the following pages is broadly considered to be a truthful and accurate account of facts and as such any inattention, use or misuse of the information in question by the reader will render any resulting actions solely under their purview. There are no scenarios in which the publisher or the original author of this work can be in any fashion deemed liable for any hardship or damages that may befall them after undertaking information described herein.

Additionally, the information in the following pages is intended only for informational purposes and should thus be thought of as universal. As befitting its nature, it is presented without assurance regarding its prolonged validity or interim quality. Trademarks that are mentioned are done without written consent and can in no way be considered an endorsement from the trademark holder.

VIP Subscriber List

Dear Reader, If you would like to receive latest tips and tricks on internet marketing, exclusive strategies, upcoming books & promotions, and more, do subscribe to my mailing list in the link below! I will be giving away a free book that you can download right away as well after you subscribe to show my appreciation!

Here's the link: http://bit.do/jonathanswalker

CONTENTS

Part 1

Introduction

Chapter 1: Prospecting – What Is It?

Chapter 2: Techniques To Use For Prospecting

Chapter 3: How To BE Prospecting In Your Prospecting

Chapter 4: Prospecting Myths

Chapter 5: Tools To Use For Prospecting

Chapter 6: Tips For Prospecting

Part 2

Chapter 1: Who Are You Talking To?

Chapter 2: What Are Your Motivations

Chapter 3: How Will You Prepare?

Chapter 4: Which Tactics Are Indispensable?

Chapter 5: The Supreme Tactic – Follow-Up Communication

Part 3

Chapter 1: How Technology Has Affected Our Communication Skills

Chapter 2: Conversation Tips

Chapter 3: Holding A Conversation

Chapter 4: Getting Through A Conversation

Chapter 5: Additional Tips

Chapter 6: After The Tips

Conclusion

Introduction

Congratulations on purchasing *The No. 1 Way to Prospect* and thank you for doing so.

The following chapters will discuss ways that you are going to be able to get new business through prospecting. Prospecting is going to be done before you are able to do any follow ups on seeing if your initial connection to the client was successful and lead to a new sale or not. There are different methods that you are going to be able to use as well as things that you should not do when it comes to prospecting, or else you are going to end up losing your business.

There are plenty of books on this subject on the market, thanks again for choosing this one! Every effort was made to guarantee it is full of as much useful information as possible; please enjoy!

Chapter one: Prospecting - What is it?

What prospecting is was briefly touched on in the introduction. When you are prospecting, you are working towards the end goal of getting potential prospects into a sale so that they become a customer that generates revenue for you.

There are some people that do not understand what the difference is between a lead and a prospect. A lead is going to be someone who is a potential customer that has to show some sort of interest in your company or the services that you offer. This can be someone who has visited your website, subscribed to your newsletter, or anything that has gotten them looking into your company.

A prospect is going to be someone who is not a lead

but is most likely going to become a customer. These are the people that you target to get them interested in your company. These are the people who have not had any interaction with your company, and if they have, then they have had limited interaction.

Ultimately, your goal is going to be the same as a lead or a prospect; you are going to want to get them to be a customer for your company.

Here is the funnel that you are going to follow to try and get a potential customer to be an actual customer.

Step one: do your research and see if you should follow the lead or let it go. You most likely have a set of criteria that you are going to go through to see how likely it is that the lead or prospect that you are looking at is going to become a customer and if you should pursue them or if you should move on to the next one. The customer relationship management software is going to be the software that you are going to use to track customers and potential customers so that you can see where they are in the sales process.

Step two: after you have determined if the lead is one that will hopefully pan out, you are going to need to connect to your target through prospecting. Someone who is in charge of contacting these leads is going to be the person that is going to reach out to them and talk to them. But, before you can reach out to them, you need to take this prospect to the person that is going to make the ultimate decision on if you should reach out to them or not. This person is typically going to be your boss, and you are most likely going to have to go through their receptionist to talk to them.

Step three: after the "decision maker" has said that it is alright, you will then either pass the information on to the next person, or you will connect to the prospect. This is going to be the initial call that you are going to make to reach out to this person and try and push them towards being a customer.

Step four: in the first call with your prospect, you are going to learn about your customer and learn what their needs are. If you think that your company can meet the needs of your prospect, then you are going to be able to move them along in the sales process. There are some things that you are going to have to fight against when it comes to getting your prospect further in the sales process. That is going to be things the prospect is going to worry about such as their budget, how long it is going to take to get the product you are offering, so on and so forth.

Step five: close your sale! Not every prospect is going to become a customer. But, when you close a won sale, you are going to have turned a prospect into a customer. However, when you have a close-lost that means that you did not get a new customer. Hopefully, your closed-won outweigh your closed-lost.

Chapter two: Techniques to Use for Prospecting

There are two main types of prospecting that you are going to do, outbound and inbound.

Outbound prospecting:

Cold calling: this will be calls that are unsolicited as you attempt to sell your product or service.

Social spamming: messages that are sent on social media that are unsolicited to sell the product or service.

When you do outbound prospecting, you are typically not going to have any contact history with the client. You are essentially trying to reach out to the person and create some connection with them that is going to put your company in their head, so when they begin to look for the product or service that you have to offer, they are going to think of you first.

Inbound Prospecting:

Warm emailing: you are going to be reaching out to someone who has expressed some kind of interest in your company before, and you want to see if there can possibly be a relationship with that person.

Social selling: social media can be used to explore relationships as well. With social media, a sales representative has the ability to answer any questions that a lead may have about the products and services that they see your company has to offer. If they cannot give the answer right there, then they can send that person in the right direction to get the answer that they are looking for.

Doing research for inbound prospecting is not going to be as extensive because the person has already interacted with your company in some way. All you are going to be doing is reaching out to that person to try and get them to spend money with your company.

It is suggested that you try and stick to inbound prospecting because most people are going to decide on if they are going to purchase a product when they hear about the product from someone that they trust. This can be from a friend of a family member, and it can be face to face or on social media.

There is a smaller amount of people who buy products because of media reports or other analyst reports.

What a lot of sales people do not realize is that whenever they "start" their sales process, they are already most of the way through it because there are not many prospects that do not have some kind of knowledge about what you are trying to sell.

In order to be successful, realize that the buyer most likely has the knowledge that you are wanting them to have. Therefore, you need to modify how you reach out to these potential buyers and rather than treat them like they do not know anything about you, educate yourself on what they do know and fill in any blanks that may be missing in the information that they already possess.

Chapter three: How to be Successful in Your Prospecting

Every company is going to have their own processes when it comes to prospecting. However, you are not going to want to become part of the sales statistic where around fifty percent of your prospecting is not productive. You are going to pick the approach that is going to work best for you and go from there. But, while you are doing that, you will have a few steps that you need to follow to be successful.

Step one: Target

You need to know who you need to talk to in order to get the sale. Too many times the contact person is going to try and start at the bottom of the company's totem pole and work their way up. This is when they tend to get stopped because you cannot get to the person that you actually need to talk to. So, before you can start contacting your prospects, you need to make sure that you have the appropriate people on that list. Your list needs to be clean and ready to go before you begin reaching out.

Step two: Value

You may have a script that you have to follow when you are talking to your prospect. But you do not have to follow it word for word. Put a personal touch to who you are speaking to. If you make a customer feel valued, then they are most likely going to spend more money with your company than if you just treat them like your company does not value them and they are just another number in your books. When you treat someone like they matter, then they are not only going to let your boss know how good you did with the sale, but they are going to request to speak to you personally when they are ready to order more product.

Step three: The right offer

Your company probably has some sort of offer that you can offer your customers. Before a customer closes a deal, they are going to want to know that they are getting the highest quality product at a reasonable price. But, interim offers that are made need to be created with care because you do not want to create an offer that causes you to lose money just for that customer.

Step four: No tricks

There is no need to cut corners when you are talking to customers. Think of it like this, if you would not tell your boss something, then do not say anything when it comes to your prospecting. Not everything has to be disclosed right up front, but you do need to be honest with your customer so that they do not feel like they are being ripped off by your company.

Step Five: Multiple touches

Often times it takes multiple tries to get ahold of someone because they are going to be busy. This usually means that many companies are having up to ten different people touch the same record before you finally get ahold of who it is that you are wanting to talk to.

Step six: Variety

Do not just stick to phone calls to your prospects. Send them mail and emails as well. While you are going to be trying to reach out to the prospect in several different ways, you need to remember to put some value in it! Look back at step two!

By following these six steps, you are going to have a higher chance of being successful when it comes to your prospecting than someone who does not.

Chapter four: Prospecting Myths

No one wants to be rejected when they are trying to make their sales. However, much like anything else, there are going to be myths that are going to surround prospecting to cause people to stray away from prospecting. Within this section of this book, you are going to learn some of the myths that surround small business prospecting.

1. Prospecting is just used for sales.

No! Prospecting is not used for sales at all. While you are prospecting, you may find someone who wants to buy from you, but that is not your goal. With prospecting, you are going to be trying to sort through the list of those that you have to reach out to and getting rid of the ones that are not interested in buying from your company. Those that are interested are going to cause the sales process to begin, but not everyone is going to want to go through this process.

2. Prospecting is nothing but a numbers game.

Many people associate prospecting with cold calls, and while cold calls are one of the prospecting techniques, you are wanting to put quality into your prospecting rather than quantity. As we discussed earlier in the book, if you make a customer feel valued, then they are most likely going to take that sales process to the next step.

3. Scripts are for kids

Scripts offer some sort of framework for how you are going to try and pull in someone when you are talking to them. You are going to have the answers to questions that they are going to be asking you. However, if you are allowed to, you can deviate from the script so that you can provide a more personalized experience for the client.

4. Prospecting is going to take time

It is not going to take you long before you know if you are going to have someone who wants to go on to the next step in the sales process or not. Not only that, but they are going to let you know if they are able to afford what it is that you are selling or not. Armed with that knowledge, you are going to be able to know when to move on and when you can keep going.

5. Close them on the appointment

Many prospects are going to agree to meet with your company because they do not want to tell you no over the phone and it is just easy to agree to meet in person than telling you no. Instead of doing this, if you think that a prospect may be interested, try a different approach such as sending them an information pack that is going to tell them more about your company and what you have to offer. If they want to move on to the next step, let them come to you!

Chapter five: Tools to Use for Prospecting

Tools for prospecting are going to make it to where you are able to manage relationships better with your prospects, and you are able to maximize your productivity. It will also assist in making sure that you do not lose track of where you are in your process with that particular customer.

Tools for your prospect list

Are you buying your list or are you creating one? Depending on your answer to that question, will depend on what tool you are going to use. When you purchase a prospect list, you are going to be taking on a lot of risk because the list is not always going to be reliable. Therefore, buying the list should be your last resort. In order to build your prospect list, you can use one of these tools.

1. Salesloft prospector: this tool is used with Google Chrome and is going to get the contact information from social media networks.
2. Broadlook capture: you are going to be able to get the information that you need about a prospect from any document or website that has any mention of them. With this information, you are going to possibly get a lot of information that is going to educate you properly on the prospect that you are looking at.
3. Data.com: this database is going to look through over a million different listings for possible prospects for you.
4. Sidekick for business: this database is going to give you around sixteen million business that you are going to be able to sort through to find

the perfect prospects for you based on what it is that you are looking for.

Managing emails

When you are using email marketing, it is going to be dependent on time. If you send out too many messages then you are going to find that you are not being found in someone's inbox due to the fact that you are pushed to the spam folder, but if you do not send out enough, you are going to be overlooked and not have any lasting impact on your prospect.

1. Sidekick for business: once again, Sidekick is going to enable you to schedule emails to send out to your prospects and get notifications whenever your website is visited by a prospect.
2. Outreach.io: the outreach tool only does one thing, but it is very good at it. With outreach, you are going to be able to set up touchpoints

for our prospects so that you can detect replies from your prospects and offers you tools where you can see when a message is converted and why it was converted.

3. Salesloft cadence: whenever you set your sales up front, you can use salesloft to set up email templates as well as reminders so that you can send out the emails whenever they need to be sent out. At the point in time that a prospect sends you an email, then that prospect will be removed from the cadence program.

4. Salesforce.com enterprise workflows: in using this tool you are going to create automatic workflows. The biggest downside to this is that it does not have many of the advanced features that other tools have to offer you.

Sales calls

Emails are not going to get all of your work done. You are going to have to call them as well, especially those that turn out to be cold leads. Most of the time it is only going to take one phone call to set up a relationship or to close a deal. But, when you combine the call with emails, you are going to be able to close even more deals because you are going to be able to get out all of the information that the client is going to need to make their decision.

1. Close.io: this program is a CRM program that is fully integrated. This is going to be the program that you use when all other programs do not fulfill what it is that you are looking for. Close.io is an all in one CRM program.
2. Ringio: with Ringio, you are going to receive a sales telephony platform that is integrated. This program is going to work with other programs such as Salesforce and Zoho so that all of our data is synced and calls are recorded in order to use them for training in making your productivity better.

Chapter six: Tips for Prospecting

These tips are going to help you in your prospecting so that if you are doing calls, you are able to crush your next call and possibly even close the deal! And, if you are new to prospecting, these tips are going to help make it to where you are one step ahead of the game.

1. Confidence! Do not let your voice waver whenever you are talking to a customer. Even if you do not know the answer to the question that they ask, do not let them know that. Simply inform them that you are going to find that answer for them. Keep in mind that they do not know who you are and they cannot see you. Besides, having confidence is going to be the number one way that you are going to close a deal.

2. Mistakes are going to happen. You are human, and you are going to make mistakes. Do not beat yourself up over this. Just move on and learn from your mistakes. There are going to be calls that are going to end up being bad, and there are going to be calls that are going to go perfectly. Do not let the bad ones keep you from moving on.

3. Know when a prospect is not a good fit. Do not continue to try and push products on a prospect that is not showing any interest in what it is that you are trying to sell. Also, if the client flat out says that they are not interested in what it is that you are promoting, thank them and move on. You do not want to keep going with a prospect when it is nothing but a dead end.

4. Be a consultant. While you are trying to sell a product, you do not have to push it on them.

Educate them instead. The sale will come later.

5. Leverage is going to improve your sales. Try and make sure that you are well aware of the marketing process of your company so that you can know what each buyer is going through when it comes to what they are looking for to meet their needs. Once you know what it is that your customer is looking for, you are going to have a better idea of what to offer them.

6. Do not be afraid to ask questions. You need to understand as much about your customer as you possibly can so that you can make sure that you are meeting their needs or moving on because they are not a good fit with your company.

7. Do not give up at the first sign of objection. You are going to come across prospects that

are going to give you excuses such as their budget. Many times these objects to see what you are going to offer them or because they want more information from you. Do not stop just because they throw up a yellow flag, offer them some more information and see if you can break through that objection.

8. Be energetic. While prospecting is going to be a tiring job, you should not let your prospect know that you are tired. Keep your energy up so that your prospect does not know what is truly going on behind the scenes. If you voice lacks enthusiasm, they are going to wonder why they should pick your company over someone else's.

PART 2

INTRODUCTION

Spoken communication, even in the digital age, still stands as the most important way in which we interact with one another. Conversations trump other forms of communications such as texts and emails because unlike these less personal, digital forms, they offer the chance to make in-game adjustments in the present moment. When we exchange ideas and express our concerns in conversation it can be something of a chess match. We want our 'moves' to ultimately create successful outcomes with the result of the conversation giving us what we hoped to accomplish. Before the conversation begins, we must give consideration to some important criteria – who it is we're talking to, what it is we want out of the conversation, and how will we prepare ourselves to have the conversation. We have to give some thought to these before considering the tactics we will employ as it is impractical to take a 'kitchen sink' approach to every conversation. The most effective conversation tactics are centered around wit, composure, politeness, consideration, flexibility, and guidance. These collectively help us to maintain quiet control over the conversation and enhance the probability that it will reach a positive conclusion. Conversations should build on one another and one way to gauge the direction of momentum is to have a brief follow-up for assurance that things are headed in the right direction.

CHAPTER 1: WHO ARE YOU TALKING TO?

For our purposes, a conversation is an exchange of verbally communicated ideas between two people. One of them is you, and the other is someone else. What is the degree of familiarity? Is it someone you've known all your life or is it that new co-worker that has been in the office for only a week? The relationship between those in the conversation helps establish a logical starting point.

An exchange between people who have only known each other professionally usually begins more formally than talk between two people who only know each other outside of their professional lives. It's appropriate to have 'small talk' precede the main focus in professional conversations due to the fact that people don't interact as often when this is the nature of the relationship and there are more uncertainties about one another.

With respect to personal relationships, there is a difference between what we shall call simple relationships and invested relationships. Because relationships have the potential to evolve, connections might be transitioning from simple to a more complex relationship such as that of a someone we've started to date or perhaps a new mother-in-law. In instances of changing connections, the capital and the stakes of conversations usually increase in value.

Certainly there are instances where two people are connected both personally and professionally, sometimes for a long period of time. Playing golf with business partners is a scenario that could lead to such a situation. This can be a little complicated, and one or both may tend to suspend the rules of engagement due to familiarity. This may require backing up and trying to have more formally constructed conversation.

If the person you're conversing with is someone new to you, it's really important to know yourself well and be aware of any personal tendencies or personality traits that might be perceived as 'a bit much' until others get to know you. Most of us can think of a personality quirk for just about anybody we know, including ourselves. Others who know us well have likely offered constructive criticism of the more challenging aspects of our personality and we should take this to heart.

CHAPTER 2: WHAT ARE YOUR MOTIVATIONS?

Any conversation has a purpose. Perhaps it is simply to maintain good relations in an established friendship. We engage in many conversations with no real purpose or objective in mind other than to maintain connection a light-hearted connection – as in the one we have perhaps with someone who we encounter once a week or so that works the check-out line in the grocery store.

Conversations don't always have a destination to be reached or some other tangible outcome, depending upon the nature of the relationship. Simple relationships such as with someone working the check-out line with who we might have a brief conversation in passing are quite different from more invested relationships, such as that with a romantic companion, relative, or professional colleague. Our motivations for engagement vary here and we need to have at least a small appreciation for the purpose, lest we lose track of what we might have invested.

Romantic and business conversations, different as they may be in terms of topics, tone, and other attributes of communication do have in common that we are talking about some level of investment on our part and presumably on the part of someone else as well. Whether it's someone we're thinking about proposing marriage or a merger, there's a lot of investment in either case.

All invested conversations require that the wants, needs, and demands of one person be measured alongside those of the other. Are you asking someone to help your business grow by offering an innovative analysis of sales data? Are you persuading your spouse that it's time for the family to grow with the addition of another child? An inventory will need to be taken in either scenario of the points that are shared in addition to where there are differences. Unless something goes terribly wrong and invested relationships dissolve, conversations will continue to occur and should reflect an effort on the part of two people to recall and maintain an awareness of what they are asking of each other.

CHAPTER 3: HOW WILL YOU PREPARE?

When a meeting is scheduled or a date is on the calendar, there is often much anticipation about how things will go. Anticipation leads to expectation or in some cases, reservation. Going over the possible outcomes in your mind followed up by a rehearsal or mock conversation is a good way to cover your bases and provide a sense of confidence about the impending conversation. If someone else is not available, read a dialogue with several exchanges as means to warm up before the actual conversation takes place

A number of variables can come into play that would affect preparation. A lot depends on whether the conversation taking place is between people in a new versus existing relationship. If the other person is new to you, other than being resourceful and gleaning some pertinent facts for conversation fodder, about all you can do is have some topics in mind in the event that the conversation stalls.

If you have the benefit of having past conversations with someone, this is helpful in that you can recall how that person tends to engage with you. Will they lead the conversation if you give them the chance or will they defer? In the cases where there is familiarity, more preparation will have to be put into a conversation that is anticipated to be strained. For instance, if conflict resolution is a likely aspect, think of appropriate questions ahead of time and ways to address issues that diffuse tension, and create a more relaxed environment. Think about acknowledging differences up front using a reconciliatory tone.

CHAPTER 4: WHICH TACTICS ARE INDISPENSABLE?

So we're at the point where introductions and small talk are over. From start to end, there are multiple tactics than can be employed to enhance the outcome, much like playing a hand of cards in a timely fashion.

Starting a conversation in amicable fashion is critical. Cut the small talk short or eliminate it if the other person is short on time or simply prefers to get down to business in short order. If it is your first conversation with someone, be mindful that you never get a second chance to make a first impression, and that impression, be it fair or not, may be formed very quickly. Early on acknowledge the other party's interests or concerns prior to stating your own, if you are the one to open things up or lead the conversation.

From start to finish, be constantly mindful and feel things out on everything from the tone of the conversation to how the other person is reacting. If a conversation gets out of hand or veers off course very far, it may be difficult to achieve the original goals that were set out. Quietly ask yourself "is everything going well, or should I try to make an adjustment?" If the other person stumbles or seems confused about how things are proceeding, try to improve clarity so that both of you are confident about how things are going relative to what might have been anticipated.

Being perceived as focused and giving the other person your full attention is perhaps the most important characteristic of someone who has productive conversations. If you come across as aloof or distracted it will probably be a downer. Someone may have taken a significant chunk of time out of their day to set aside for what they thought was going to be a meaningful exchange and instead they are totally deflated by someone who seems somewhere else.

We have already shed light on coming up with appropriate questions in advance for what are anticipated to be challenging conversations. This is particularly true if modern electronic communication or social media exchanges have preceded or led to the conversation. Incomplete thoughts or confusion created by these shorthand approaches to communicating may result in questions that should be dealt with at the beginning of the conversation. Heck, they may be the entire reason for the conversation. Giving prior thought to appropriate questions is good in any case as the most relevant questions may not come to mind if you wait until the conversation has begun. It is likely that the most curious questions, which reflect serious thought on your part, will come up in advance. Modify questions if you perhaps initially asked something too broad.

Maintain composure rather than get defensive when someone is confrontational or insulting. Disarming someone with a witty or playful response give you the control that they forfeited by deploying counterproductive language.

Give thorough responses that indicate you have respect for other peoples' questions. Abbreviated or literal responses in addition to being insufficiently clear, may also suggest a lack of respect or consideration for what the other person is trying to learn. If their facial expression or other observable response suggests that they did not get the information they were wanting, politely ask them to clarify what they were asking for if it is not abundantly clear.

Be mindful of where the conversation is going and be ready to get it back on track if it is headed into unproductive or counterproductive turf. Be prepared to usurp the role of leading the conversation should it stall. The other person might not be inclined to take the initiative here, and you may have no way of knowing if they're new to you.

Just like you shouldn't give a literal or abbreviated response, you shouldn't ask questions that would lead someone to think you were asking for such. Questions that demand responses beyond the mundane will give the other person a chance to share a more detailed account leaving them feeling as though they got to share the whole story.

People want to be recognized and given due credit.

Do yourself a favor and take the opportunity in advance. If they feel the need to bring attention to an accomplishment before you mention it, they are indicating that they feel a lack of respect. Recognition will make future conversations more productive because validation will motivate people to be more engaged.

We need to listen effectively in order to gain the respect of those we engage in conversation. Constantly cutting them off or interrupting them will make it seem as we are dismissing their importance in the relationship. One is not listening effectively if they are unable to stay in the present moment. Diverting the conversation may also be regarded as not respecting someone's concern about the topic at hand.

Making demands or requests in a conversation is a sensitive matter. Be fair and don't ask for too much. Don't ask for something if it is going to be obvious that you haven't done anything to help yourself and just want to place a burden on the other person. No one wants to feel as though they're being taken advantage of, so consider carefully as to whether you should make a request of them.

Demonstrate that you are in the moment by actions that are visibly obvious. Record notes during the conversation or commitments you have made. Place a future date on your phone calendar when an event is mentioned. This implies intent on your part to follow through and makes the other person feel as though they've gotten something across to you and that their input was worthwhile.

CHAPTER 5: THE SUPREME TACTIC - THE FOLLOW-UP CONVERSATION

After a conversation, you must take inventory of how things went. If you know of strategic mistakes that were made along the way, make note of them and take care not to commit them in future conversations. You must hold yourself responsible for being able to recall any specific outcomes and good note-taking is the best way to accomplish this. If a conversation ends with both parties knowing what was specifically agreed to or are certain of specific commitments that were made and how outcomes are to be achieved, it may not be necessary to revisit the conversation down the road. When outcomes aren't certain and nothing was specifically agreed upon, it may be in the best interest of two people to come back together and express their views about what each took from the conversation. Revisit the points of agreement and disagreement with emphasis given as to why sentiments differed on particular subjects that were discussed. An apologetic tone might be called for if you lost your composure or you felt deficient in attention or focus. Remember that follow-up conversation may be used as a polite gesture to offer thanks or appreciation, in which case they needn't be extended affairs. If a follow-up is something of an in-between linking two major conversations, it may require more input as it establishes what will be discussed in the latter conversation.

PART 3

Chapter 1

How Technology Has Affected Our Communication Skills

Before we dive into the practical strategies of overcoming those dreaded awkward moments, there is some basic information that you should know. You see, it is my belief that seeing a full picture of the context will help you to understand the basis of your communication block better.

In truth, the world we live in today is a lot different than it used to be back in the days of covered wagons and community bathing. Yuck! It is certainly better in a myriad of ways. We have the technology, fast cars, airplanes, hell even indoor plumbing! But. Just but. It isn't better in some respects.

We Were Set Up To Fail

You see, people call this the age of communication. People call this the golden era of instant connectivity based on the ease in which we can talk to people hundreds or even thousands of miles away from us. That is certainly a great thing in all but wait. What about the people that are sitting right next to us? How connected to them are we?

Over seventy percent of the world's population admits to having a problem with communicating properly with people in their families. Think about that for a moment. SEVENTY

PERCENT! That is just mind boggling. And to put things into perspective, more than three out of four of your neighbors probably face this same issue as you do.

It is also faithful to a vast extent that a consequence of that problem leads to one not having the proper communication skills to engage on a personal level with strangers or primary acquaintances.

Have you noticed that in the past, before telephones were in every household, it was so much easier to talk to people face to face? That is because for the longest time, excluding the post that came every week or the occasional messenger pigeon that often took days to reach a destination seventy miles away, it was the **only** form of communication with someone! If you wanted to have a full conversation in real time with someone you knew that wasn't living in your own home you had to move your butt up from your seat, walk over to their house, knock on their door, open your mouth, and talk to them. Sounds harsh eh? Now think how many people do that now in the modern age.

This meant that communication was futile to survival in the past. If you needed something from someone, you had to physically and verbally ask for it. This also meant that you would have to communicate regularly with everyone around you to get stuff done.

Past Customs Allowed For Natural Conversations

In the past, it was customary to greet everyone with a smile when you're walking down the street. Not doing so was considered bad manners. In contrast, people living in the modern age are so glued to their smartphones or listening to their music with earphones shoved deep down their ear drums that their mouths don't even move much anymore. People are LESS connected to one another today.

In the past humans had to interact by speaking several times a day and as a result, people were not only more friendly to one another, they became more fluent and natural at talking and communicating with their peers. They had proper training on a daily basis just by opening their mouths more often. How easy is that?

We Were Not Given The Chance To Develop Our Social Skills

You see, children in days gone by were taught from a young age how to socialize. They were sent outside to make their friends, and they were taught how to be self-sufficient. This gave them the confidence to speak to others. In school, they were instructed on what appropriate conversation was. Children were often taught not to speak unless spoken to. This was to teach them to listen to those around them truly and to respond in a meaningful and understanding way. This training not only made them good listeners but also compassionate adults that were able to hold productive conversations in the highest of social settings. As you can see, a conversation was key to survival.

Where's The Social Gathering In The Modern Age?

Let's face it. We are all glued to our smartphones, tablets, and computers. Swiping left on Tinder, surfing the net, texting people on Facebook or iMessage. When have we ever had a decent conversation or a happy get-together with our closest friends? The truth is that we were crippled by our devices the day we got them. It is unfortunate now, isn't it?

Consequences Of Rapid Development

The hectic life and "connectivity" today has turned our society a complete one hundred and eighty degrees. We have started to take for granted the most straightforward and efficient tools for communication and replaced them with devices that we THINK are doing a better job for us. In reality people today are more closed off than they ever were and that is unfortunate. Modernization and technology have robbed us of our most core competencies, and we need to claim it back!

The Intricate Things We ARE Deprived Of:

The gatherings with friends and family

The lack of fun festivities

The missing social events

The community spirit and comradery with our peers.

The treatment of everyone around you with respect and dignity that you wish you received.

The Communication with our neighbors.

Possible Causes

There are many possible reasons for this silence struck pandemic. Most of it can be attributed to one or more of the many technological advances that we have seen over the years. No one person has been able to pinpoint exactly what it is that has changed the friendly ways of the world. Here are some of the possible causes. You can try to decide for yourself what you think has been the downfall of communication.

- The Telephone: The invention of the phone made it easier to take the human element out of a conversation. Instead of going to someone's house every so often and staying a few hours, and having a meal, they could call to say what needed to be said, and then cut the conversation short with the excuse that they were wracking up too many minutes that month. They didn't have to stay on the phone yacking for hours on end because the person on the other end of the line agreed and hung up as well.

The telephone, back when it was invented, was so expensive that only the rich people and government agencies owned them. Created in 1876 by Alexander Graham-Bell, it was the most technologically advanced thing since the dawn of electricity. In the beginning, it cost over a thousand dollars to own a single phone. To make a call, Bell Telephone Industries charged a dollar a minute to dispatch that call. That was a lot of money considering the average worker was lucky to make fifty cents an hour. One minute call time would have been two hours wages, so most average salary households did not have a telephone in the house. That was until the early 1900's after Henry Ford invented the concept of mass production. A company made a telephone that was way cheaper than Bell Industries old phone design, and they found a better way to dispatch calls to make the calls cheaper. During this time, wages went up a lot as well. By this period the minimum wage was about two dollars an hour. This made phones more common in average households. By the nineteen seventies, a home phone was a staple in each house and calls only cost ten cents a minute. This was a great thing, as, by this time, wages were up to seven dollars an hour for minimum wage. The company that was instrumental in lowering the price of the phone? Well, these days it's known as AT&T.

Due to its cost, the telephone may not have been the downfall of modern communication, but it definitely could have had a hand in it. Particularly as it became easier, and cheaper to purchase. People called rather than stopped by, and these calls did not have to drone on and on, as time was money. This allowed conversations to become shorter, and it made its way into everyday life as well.

- Television: The television was a lot cheaper than the telephone was. It was also a way to get the news a lot easier, as you didn't have to wait until a friend heard something and get back to you. There were also some good programs to watch during the day that entertained people. This entertainment made them want to stay inside and watch it all day. Well, the adults at least. Children were still sent outside to play.

The original television was black and white and only had three channels. It was small and could sit on the dining room table. Brand new, they cost about three hundred dollars, and they had long rabbit ear antennas. In the beginning, this was the only option you had, but as time went on, there were bigger console televisions available. Eventually, the color television was introduced, and some time after that, more channels were added, as cable became a thing. More and more time was spent inside watching TV. Not just by adults anymore, either. Children were inside more often and watched shows that were geared towards their age groups. People went out and mingled with their neighbors less and less.

Television alone probably was not the downfall of the

communication era, but it was a precedent to it. A lot of people began staying inside to watch their soaps instead of going outside to spend time with actual people. For the longest time, children were still sent out to play while the parents watched TV, but as the parents moved to colored cable, the children got the still working black and white rabbit-eared television, and the trend progressed as in the older days, television sets lasted forever.

- Game Consoles: Today there are several hi-tech game consoles out there for people to choose from, and they are often played for hours on end, while the player ignores the outside world. Back when they were first invented, they were a lot different, but no less desirable. They were the envy of every household, and a child that had one was instantly familiar, but he never used that popularity because he was too busy inside playing his new game. When the original Atari came out, it was the sensation that swept the nation.

The first ever game console was nothing like the ones we have today. They took a lot more effort to play. To make a single move, you had to write a program first. This was difficult, but the kids in those days didn't mind, as to them it was a game console, and that was the coolest thing they had ever seen. They also learned about computer programming before home computers were a thing. As time progressed, the programs were written into the game at production, so all kids had to do was play the game. They also went from almost fifteen hundred dollars to a hundred and fifty dollars. While that was still pretty expensive, it was a lot more affordable than the Atari. The most popular and innovative of these new consoles? The Nintendo Entertainment System, or NES for short. It was the console that every kid wanted, and most kids were able to get for Christmas or their birthday. With the debut of the game Super Mario Brothers stepping away from the typical games of Pong and Galactica, this thrilling console had kids of all ages, and even adults gathered around it to enjoy it. This further engulfed them into their anti-social bubbles as they were too engrossed in the games to go outside.

Video Games are blamed by many as being the downfall of modern society. That can be seen as accurate, as there were so many people beginning to stay indoors rather than going outside. However, there were plenty of friendly people left in the world, and people still visited one another, so is this the truth? Maybe as they progressed, but it was not an immediate destruction.

- Media: This one can be brutal. People are so easily influenced by the media, that they could tell the people that Donald Trump farted unicorns, and they would almost believe it. Okay, maybe not that sorry, but that is the general idea with the media. Nowadays, the media is filled with bombings, kidnappings and other fear mongering materials that it makes it hard to trust the people around you.

In the beginning, the news just stated that. The news. It gave news of the war if there was one, and news With all the fear-inducing news, it makes it hard to want to even talk to anyone, because it seems as if everyone is a murderer now. This is not a conducive environment like friendly ways of the past.

Media could be considered the downfall of the friendly atmosphere, as it seeds fear of the human race in your mind, and that is what seems to have closed people off from their natural chatty instincts.

- Internet: The dawn of the web saw a rise in introverts massively. It is no secret that the web has taken over the minds of most of our youth. This goes hand in hand with the media, as it is the primary source of all media output.

So those are some of the possible causes of why it is harder now to talk to people than it used to be. Of course, for some people, it is more difficult than others. Individuals with anxiety or shyness have a hard time even talking to people that are deemed safe by people they trust. It isn't caused by fear, just a nervousness that causes these people to clam up. Chances are since you are reading this, you are one of these people.

Do not fret. This book will help you get through this. However, be prepared. Sometimes it takes more than self-help, and if your problem has deeper seated issues, you may want to get the help of a psychiatrist. If these tips do not help, it is best to seek the help of one if you wish to be more of a conversationalist, and it is essential for your mental and emotional health. There will be more on that at the end of this book.

Chapter 2
Conversation Tips

Step One-Talking to Yourself

This may seem a little silly, but it does help. It is the easiest way to get over your shyness, as it is more awkward to talk to yourself than it is to talk to other people. You just have to get past the first hump of not wanting to look like a fool and own it.

Go into a room with a mirror, start by offering your hand to shake and mime shaking hands with the person staring back at you while introducing yourself. This may feel a little weird, as there is not going to be a meeting of hands, due to you only having the conversation with yourself.

Once you get past the standard greeting, it is time to hold a conversation. You can either say your mirrored self's responses, or you can keep them in your head. This is where it can get tricky. You cannot think of specific to you answers, rather, you have to think of general answers, as you are not the person you are talking to. Talk away as if an actual person was holding a conversation with you. You can think of this as a live diary, but more civilized and social, as you don't want to spill your secrets to someone who is mostly standing in as a stranger.

Here is a little scenario to help you visualize what it would be like.

SCENARIO

Kelly had just finished reading *How to Talk to Anyone: Ten Secrets You Wish You Knew*, and she wanted to try out the first tip, which was called "Talking to Yourself." She stepped into her bathroom and closed the door.

"Okay, Kelly. You can do this. You have to become better at holding a conversation, as your husband's job requires you to attend various social events with him."

Looking into the mirror she offered her hand to the cold glass, feeling slightly foolish.

"Hello, my name is Kelly. And you are?"

In her head, she planned the response.

I am Richard Simms. A pleasure to meet you, Kelly. She used her husband's boss's name as that was the one she was sure she knew.

"Pleasure to meet you too, sir. How are you and your wife and kids?"

They are doing well, as am I. How about your children?

"Oh, no children yet sir. Wanting to get ahead financially first."

A great plan, I must say. Children are very expensive little buggers.

Kelly was interrupted then, as her husband walked into the bathroom.

"Who on Earth are you talking to?"

"I am practicing holding a conversation. I don't want to embarrass you tomorrow at the banquet." Kelly blushed.

"Awe, sweetheart, you could never embarrass me, but I appreciate the effort, and I am glad you are taking the steps necessary to better yourself. I am proud of you." Her husband kissed her forehead and left.

After that boost of confidence, Kelly found it much easier to practice her conversation skills and felt less awkward about talking to herself in the mirror.

It may seem embarrassing to talk to yourself in a mirror, but after awhile it will be much easier, as you will start to feel better about helping yourself become the best that you can be. If someone comes in and asks you what you are doing, explain to them what you are trying to do. You never know, maybe they will try it for themselves.

Of course, there is still a stigma that talking to yourself means that you are crazy, but once you explain that you are not trying to be weird, you just are trying to become better at conversation, people will understand. It is getting harder and harder for people to hold a normal conversation in this world, so it is always refreshing to hear that someone is trying to better themselves.

Step Two- Have a Few Ice Breakers

It is no secret that after the initial introductions conversation gets awkward if there are no real conversation starters in the room. You say hello, state your name, and ask a few questions about what the person does, and how their day has been, but after that is over, this is when the conversation dies out with a bunch of "Ums" and "Uhhh." Having a few icebreakers is always important as you can keep the conversation going, and often have a few laughs going at the end.

Of course, it is hard to tell exactly what you should use as an icebreaker, and that is why most people have a hard time keeping the conversation going. However, few foolproof icebreakers will make talking to someone a breeze. This section will go over some ice breakers to use... and some to avoid.

Real Ice Breakers

- Latest viral cat video: Pretty much everyone in the world loves cat videos, and a lot of people have seen them. Bringing that up in conversation is always a good way of push conversation along. It is a safe topic that won't offend people, and if someone hasn't seen the video, you can show it to them, eliciting a few laughs and smiles. Almost everyone loves cat videos.

- Food: Everyone eats. So ask the person what kind of food they like. It is always pertinent to ask them first because if they are vegan, you don't want to say "Bacon is the greatest, is it not?" Discuss different cuisines, and if they have not tried one of your favorites, suggest a good place find it. Talking about food can bring people closer together, as they find common likes and interests in cuisines.

- Music: Everyone listens to music. No matter what their tastes, everyone loves music. You cannot deny the fact that life would be boring without it. It fills the awkward silences, and it can bring up someone who is down. There is no escaping the fact that music is tied to emotions as well. Try asking the person what their favorite song is. Ask them the genres they like. If you find you have some interests that are similar, that is great, and that will further boost the conversation.

- Hobbies: Everyone has a passion that probably has nothing to do with their job. Hobbies are what make life interesting. It is a safe topic to approach because many people love to talk about what they enjoy, but rarely anyone asks.

- Anything to do with interests: Pretty much anything to do with personal interests is safe to talk about because people love to talk about themselves. They like to make known what they enjoy, and they love when someone shows interest in them. However, most people are too shy to talk about themselves unprompted because they do not wish to seem conceited.

Bad Ice Breakers

- Politics: There are so many different opinions out there, and unfortunately with the policy, everyone thinks that they are right. The conversation can get awkward if you are a Democrat butting heads with a Republican. That is only the tip of the iceberg though. Tempers often flare at the slightest mention that either party may be corrupt, so it is best all around to just avoid the conversation entirely.

- Religion: This is another one that is best avoided. Religion is a very sensitive subject for some, and no one wants someone else's religion shoved in their faces. That is why you are better off keeping this one put away.

- Life choices: It is great that you have decided to become a vegan and all, but you do not have to convert everyone who is around you. Same with any of the life choices you make, whether you sell Avon or those scammy weight loss products, virtually no one wants to hear the spiel. Save it for if you are asked.

So there you have it. Some good and some not-so-good icebreakers to help you extend any conversation past the initial hello. Once you can establish a gateway to the conversation, you will be able to carry on a lot easier than you would if you had not used an icebreaker at all, and were floundering about like a fish out of water, trying to figure out what to say.

How These Tips Help

These tips help you relax a little bit. They give you a little confidence boost, knowing that you are prepared to hold a conversation with people you may meet because you have practiced the basics. It is a lot easier to do something once you have practiced it a few times.

It also helps you get past the awkwardness, as nothing is more awkward than holding a conversation with yourself. You will be able to talk to someone without feeling silly because you couldn't possibly feel any goofier than you did speak to a mirror.

Follow these tips to get the ball rolling on talking to people.

Chapter 3
Holding a Conversation

Now that you have gotten past the tips on how to approach and talk to someone, it is time to move on to the advice on how to hold a conversation. This is important because starting a conversation is only a small part of the battle. This means that you have to be able to continue a conversation past the point of the icebreaker.

Conversations do not have to be hours long, but you do have to keep them at a length that does not make you seem rude, or disinterested. If you only talk to someone about one subject and then leave, the person will feel as if they did something to offend you or something like that. You do not want to leave anyone feeling that way.

The best way to avoid that is to make sure that you keep the conversation going to the point where it would be safe to exit without offending the person you are talking too. This section will help you more understand how to keep a conversation going and keep it going well.

Tip Three- Self Disclosure

To understand this advice, there is going to have to be some in-depth explanation of what self-disclosure is. To save you from having to look it up, this tip will include all the information you need to know about it. Of course, that will make this trip a lot longer, but it is better to have a long tip that you understand than a short briefing on something that leaves you confused.

Self-disclosure is where you add to a conversation by giving the other person information about yourself. This is a hard thing to do, as most people worry about boring others with talk of themselves, or they are afraid to seem conceited.

There are two dimensions to self-disclosure. They are breadth and depth. These are both essential to holding a good conversation, and connecting with the person you are talking to. You want to be able to connect with the people around you or else you will not be able to hold a genuine and meaningful conversation. You have to have both to enable the act of self-disclosure indeed.

The breadth of self-disclosure refers to the range of topics you discuss when opening up about yourself. No, you don't have to disclose your deepest darkest secrets, but giving someone a little bit of information about several different subjects about yourself allows them to feel a little closer to you, thus enabling them to open up about themselves. This helps extend the conversation and lets the person feel values as if you are interested in talking with them. Try starting with the easiest topics, such as interests, and move on to schooling, and views on the world. The more subjects you cover, the longer the conversation will be, and the more you will be able to connect with the person you are talking too.

Depth is slightly harder to reach. Now if you are just chatting up with someone you don't plan to develop a deep friendship with, you can almost skip depth, but a deep conversation is necessary for those you wish to establish a real friendship with. However, even in a simple conversation, you need to have some depth to what you are saying. Tell them about the time you broke your arm in third grade, or something of the like. Give them a memory to make them feel as if you care about the conversation you are having, and are not just chatting to pass the time.

The act of self-disclosure is a type of social penetration. This is a theory that you can only establish any relationship, whether it be romantic or platonic, by communication. But not just any type of communication, systematically fluid conversation. This means that over time, you let the person in more and more, and you change the direction of your conversation regularly to establish a connection with the individual you are communicating with.

You also have to allow time for the person to reciprocate in the conversation. Don't spend the entire time talking about yourself. If you are worried about droning on too long about what you like and such, try employing the one detail method. This means that you share a detail about yourself, and let the other person share a detail about themselves. Continue this on until you find a happy medium between not sharing enough and talking too much.

As you can see self-disclosure is critical, as you need to allow, a person to feel as if you are invested in the conversation. If you do not seem like you care to talk to them, they will close off, and not want to talk much more than the basic hello followed by an icebreaker subject. So how do you efficiently employ this technique?

- Start Small: On top of them feeling like you are interested, they also have to be interested in what you have to say. Rather than unloading a whole pile of information on someone that doesn't care, start with a small bit of information to see if they take the bait. If you use the icebreaker about music, try telling them your favorite song, and explaining a final reason for why you love it. If they just give you a one-word reply, it is best to duck out of the conversation then. They don't care. However, if they seem interested, and ask you, more then you can start talking about more of your interests and such.

- Decide on The Type of Conversation: You should always try to approach every conversation as if you seek to make a new friend. However, if you are at a convention with people from around the globe, chances are you are not going to establish a life-long friendship. You should still show interest in the individual, but that would impact the type of information that you are going to divulge. You don't want someone you are never going to see again knowing a deep secret about you. Instead, tell them about childhood memories that you don't feel would impact how they think of you. Your favorite thing to do as a child or stuff like that. Those are safe subjects for people who you are just talking to at that moment.

- Skim the Surface: You want people to be interested in you for a long time. This means that you cannot divulge everything about you in one conversation. You have to be conservative with your information. The best way to do this is to take a little bit of information from many different subjects to talk about. As you get to know a person more and more, you can add more details to that. This helps you also ensure that you are not talking about yourself too much.

- Allow Reciprocation: The best part of self-disclosure is that it allows the other person a gateway to say themselves as well. You don't want to hog the stage and only talk about yourself. You want to keep the flow of information even. Give the other person some time to tell you about themselves as well. The conversation will come alight as you are swapping stories and some fun little tidbits of information about yourself.

- Be Loose: Telling someone about yourself should be done with ease. You don't want to sound like someone who is selling something, though in reality that is what you are doing in a way. You are trying to convince the person to like you with the truth. However, it should not sound like you are a documentary. You should be light and airy when talking about yourself. Make the person interested. Intrigue them, and draw them in, get them want to know more about you.

- Timing: Just like when you deliver the punchline to a joke, it is all about the timing. You have to time the information that you provide. This is a little tricky if you don't know what goes into timing a deliverance. There has to be a level of interest from the other person. To ensure that you have their interest, you have to make them ask a few questions. You can't just offer up all the information. However, you can't make them pry every bit of info from you either. There has to be a give and take kind of flow going on there.

- Caution: There are some things that you do not tell a person you just met. It may seem like you have known the person forever, but you still have to use caution when divulging certain things. For example, if you were a former addict, it is best not to mention it unless necessary. You do not want anything to skew how they think of you until they get to know you. If you are confident in yourself, however, then try divulging that info. What you are cautious with depends on you.

There you have it. Self-disclosure at its finest. This is one of the most important things to holding a good conversation. Now, remember, your entire conversation does not have to consist of self-disclosure alone, but throwing in a few facts here and there go a long way. Make sure you utilize this to the fullest advantage possible.

Tip Four- Engage the Other Person Fully

Part of the problem these days is that conversation becomes one sided. Even though both parties are speaking, they are not really in the conversation. They are not properly engaging the other person. This is a big issue when communication relies entirely on both parties being actively involved in the discussion to allow it to succeed. If you are not actively engaging the other person, and not participating yourself, then you will fall flat in the conversation.

First off, how you can be engaged in the conversation better, without taking it over.

- Actively Listen: No one wants to feel like they are talking to a brick wall. They want to feel like the person they are talking to is genuinely interested in what they have to say. This means that you have to listen to understand. Today's generation teaches you to hear the reply, and that is where the problem lies. By only looking to respond, you are not processing what the other person is saying because your mind is on yourself. This is a selfish, bad habit that this day and age has taken to sticking too.

- Reply with Interest: Even if you are not quite interested in what the other person is talking about, you should always respond with interest. It is polite, and even though you may not be interested in it now, you might gain some interesting knowledge by listening to what they have to say. You can't just expect everyone to have the same interests as you, and there are probably things that you like that others do not like but they still act like they are at least interested in it, because it is the polite thing to do.

- Ask Questions: Asking questions to get more information about what they are talking about shows the other person that you were listening, and that you want to know more. It allows the person to be relieved because then they do not feel like they are boring you with their information. The only way that they know that you are interested is if you are asking questions.

Then they know that it is okay to continue talking about the subject they are on.

- Be THERE: I know it can be hard if someone is droning on and on about something that you have no interest in, but it is still good etiquette to be there mentally. This means that when someone is talking, don't let your mind go on vacation, and tune the person out because if you are that disinterested in them, it is more polite to change the subject rather than just leave the conversation mentally.

That is how you can be engaged in a conversation. Following these tips will allow you to breathe easier knowing that you are pleasantly talking to a person, and you won't offend them because you seem disinterested. You just have to practice these things, because sometimes it can be a little tricky.

How to Engage Them

- Be Interesting: This does not mean you have to make up stories. It has nothing to do with the information you are giving at all. You just have to deliver it in an interesting way. You could tell someone you climbed Mount Everest on the back of Dwayne Johnson, and if you inform the story in a monotone voice, it will sound dull. It is not what you are saying; it is how you are saying. Tell them your stories as if you were telling them for the first time. Be engaged yourself, and show the person that you want them to talk to you. You want their attention. Only then will you get the attention you so desire.

- Leave Openings: Even without using self-disclosure, you still have to leave openings for the other person to talk, no matter the subject. No one wants to stand there and listen to someone take control of the conversation. You might as well be talking to yourself for that matter. Or to the plant in the corner. You have to let the other person talk as well. A good conversation allows both parties to talk equally and without any hitches. It is not people talking about everything while the other person stands there and nods.

- 🎬 Allow Questions: If a person asks a question, don't dodge it. This should not have to be said, but a lot of people avoid questions for fear of sounding conceited, but in truth, you just seem rude. If someone is asking a question, you are not going to sound pretentious by answering it. If you dodge a question, the person will feel as if they offended you, and they will be less likely to stay engaged in the conversation.

That is how you engage someone in conversation. It is a lot easier than staying involved in a discussion as long as they are interested in what is being said. All you have to do is be open and friendly, and let the rest fall into place.

How These Tips Help

These tips are designed to help you keep a conversation going without being nervous. These tips also contribute to improving your communication skills. By using these tips, you will feel more comfortable having a longer conversation with someone that you just met than you would be if you were just trying to find things to talk about.

These tips will give you the boost you need to feel confident in your abilities to talk to people and enjoy the conversation without having to worry every second that you are saying something wrong.

Chapter 4
Getting Through a Conversation

These tips are for what you should do during and after a conversation with someone. They are tips on how to properly act when communicating, as there is often some confusion about what to do especially now that it is no longer a curriculum at school or home. Do not fret. This book will clarify that right up.

Tip Five- Etiquette During a Conversation

It is of utmost importance that you have the proper etiquette when talking to someone. The key to holding a good conversation is not to offend them and to show them that you are a real person to talk to. You want to keep their attention and let them know that they have yours. Otherwise, you will not get very far in the communication realm, as people will not want to talk to you, thinking you are rude.

So it is best to study up on proper etiquette before you put yourself out there. While most of these are common sense, they are in here just in case nerves cause a problem with combining common sense with communication. That is a real issue a lot of people have. They cannot rely on their common sense because they are too nervous to remember to use it.

So here are the etiquette rules to help you out. Remember, a slip up is okay as long as you don't do it continually, but it is best to try to be as clean cut as possible to avoid any issues.

- Handshake: This is the first thing you should do, as you say hello. Unless the person is germaphobic, or you are, not offering a handshake is considered rude. If you do have a phobia of germs, it is best to explain that as you are saying hello, so there are no misunderstandings. Make sure that they know that you are still pleased to meet them; you just would rather not shake their hand. Most people can be pretty understanding.

  The perfect handshake is firm but pliant. You can't

grip too tight, because you are not trying to intimidate someone, and a grip too loose makes people feel that you are not that thrilled to meet them, and are only doing so out of necessity. This is not a great first impression, as people want to feel like they are worth getting to know. So it is best to make sure you give a real, genuine handshake.

- Eye Contact: This one is important to maintain from the beginning to end. It is always disconcerting to talk to someone who is looking off into the distance or anywhere else but who is talking to them. (autistic people are not counted in this, nor are the ocularly impaired) Eye contact shows that you are paying attention to them. To show you why eye contact is so important, let us have a mini history lesson.

Back in the time of extreme social hierarchy, where people who made less money than you were deemed undesirable, eye contact was a way of establishing that social ladder. Anyone who was considered below you had to make eye contact with you, while you were not to make eye contact with them. To make eye contact with a person deemed lowly, put you on their level, and could cause you to lose your social position if caught.

Kings never looked anyone but other kings in the eye, no one ever made eye contact with serfs other than other serfs. Men did not make eye contact with women, as even women were deemed below them. They only time someone made eye contact with a lady that was not another woman, was a servant, or a peasant to a duchess or queen. Eye contact was the primary factor of social hierarchy

By not looking someone in the eye during a conversation, you are essentially saying that they are beneath you and that what they have to say is n't matter. That may not be what you are trying to do, but that is the message you are portraying when you refuse to look someone in the eye.

- Body Language: This will be more brushed on in a later chapter, but it also falls under etiquette. You have to have an open body language in a conversation. Otherwise, you risk making a person feel as if you are unapproachable, and not open to discussion. You can also make them feel as if what they are saying has no value. You can do so much damage with a few simple gestures, and this is a problem. You have to be careful with your stance and make sure that you are not closing yourself off.

- No Phone: This should go without saying, but if your phone goes off, DON'T ANSWER IT! Society today is so caught up in the conversations that they have going on on the other side of the screen, that they forget the importance of conversation with the person on the other aspect of the table. You are in a real time conversation with a real person. (Not that the person texting you isn't real, but they are not there.) The best thing to do is to put your phone on silent if you know you are going to talk to people. That way you do not feel tempted to pull it out and text rather than speaking with those around you.

Cell phones are a wonderfully destructive device. They can help you connect with people from around the world, but unfortunately, that causes you to disconnect from the people that are right next to you. A lot of people use their phone as a crutch to not have to talk to people when they feel uncomfortable. This does not help you in any way. They only way to become comfortable with a situation is to put yourself out there and talk to people. Find someone to talk to and eventually you will take your mind off of the fact that you are anxious about being around people.

- Don't Interrupt: When someone is talking to you, it is best to stay quiet until you are sure they have finished what they are saying. You have to be very careful when talking to someone that you are listening to them, and not listening to respond. This is one of the biggest problems in today's conversations. No one looks to people for more than knowing when to jump in and reply. This leads to more people interrupting, which often angers the other person, and makes them not want to talk to you any longer.

Listen to the person, and remember that you would not want to be interrupted. No one likes to be talked over, and no one likes talking to someone who constantly does it. Be patient. Your time to talk will come.

- Personal Space: This is a big one. A lot of people get really close to people when they are talking. This is uncomfortable for the other person. You have to make sure that you keep a safe distance between you and the other person. Arm's length apart is a good chatting distance unless you are in a loud place, and then from forearm length apart is usually as close as you should be. If it is too loud to hear, then you should hold the conversation until you are in a quieter environment.

Claustrophobia is a big problem for a vast majority of a population. Invading someone's personal space can make them very uncomfortable. You have to respect that people need personal space when talking to you. Even if they don't have claustrophobia, it is still gross when someone is so close to you that you can feel their spit as they are talking. Keep the distance.

- Get Close: This may seem to contradict the last statement, but you have to be close enough that it does not look like you are trying to escape the conversation. However, it is not that contradictory. You just have to find a happy medium. You want to be close enough that the other person is not sniffing themselves trying to figure out if it is them, but you have to be far enough away that you are not crowding their personal space.

A good indicator is your arms. Of course, you do not physically stretch them out to see if you are standing close enough, but rather you visualize where you are at. You should never be so close that you have to bend your arm at more than a ninety-degree angle to touch them, but you should not be so far away that when your arms are fully outstretched your palms can't rest on their shoulders. Try to stay in that golden circle of space, and you should be good.

Those are the tips for etiquette during a conversation. Follow these, and you should have no problem with people not wanting to talk to you. You will make the other person feel respected, and that is what you are striving for.

Tip Six- Etiquette When Leaving a Conversation

- Timing: As stated before, timing is everything when talking to people. You have to be good at your timing and actually, know when to say something when not to say something. In this case, timing has to do with when to exit a conversation. No matter how good a conversation has been, you begin to wear out your welcome. If a person starts to look around or shift about, they are probably ready to go or do something else. This is your cue to end the conversation if they do not. Finish what you were saying, and then use an exit phrase such as "Oh I can't believe how much of your time I have taken! It was so great talking to you I just got swept up at the moment!" Make them feel good while ending the conversation.

- Ending Phrase: As mentioned in the above bullet, you have to use a good ending phrase to make the person feel as if the conversation end is not their fault, even if it is. Be polite, and make them feel like you were so enthralled by talking to them that you regret having to end the conversation, but you do not want to take up any more of their time. This will make them feel valued, and that will get them want to talk to you again.

- Ask for Contact Info: If you have the chance of seeing someone again, or just would like to stay in touch, ask if they would like to exchange contact information. If they say yes, go ahead and give them your number and ask for theirs, giving a test call to make sure you input the number right and allowing them to be sure of the same, as the will have your number on the call. If they do not wish to exchange information, do not push. It doesn't mean you did anything wrong; they just may not think that they will see you again. That is okay.

Always ask if they want to exchange information. It is a lot more comfortable for them, as it gives them a little more room to say no without feeling bad. Asking them for their contact information directly does not allow for them to say no without feeling bad because you assumed that they wanted to. Remember, the right conversation does not mean they have to become your best friend. A lot of people get so attached to someone they had a single enthralling conversation with, that they are upset when the person does not want to keep in touch. This is only human nature, as we are designed to communicate for survival.

Breaking yourself of this habit will be difficult, but if you do it, you will be less affected by the rejection you feel when someone does not wish to stay in touch.

- Follow Up: This only refers to people who exchanged info. If they give you their contact information, then text or call them the next day to see how they are doing and let them know that you were serious about wanting to stay in touch. Make the person feel important, but only text once, and let them respond. They might be busy when you try to reach them and will get back to you later.

These are the etiquette rules for ending a conversation. If you use them, you can be confident that you are not leaving someone with awkwardness in the air.

How These Tips Help

These tips give you the boost up in a conversation to show a person that you are respectful, and that you have proper manners. This will make them enjoy talking to you a lot better than if you did not know these rules.

Etiquette is slowly slipping away, by trying to bring it back, you will also start a ripple effect, as the person you are talking to will pick up on these social cues, and start using them in their conversations with others. By doing this little simple thing, you can help bring proper communication etiquette back into a trend.

Chapter 5

Additional Tips

These tips are just extra tips that you should know and insert throughout different conversations. They do not necessarily have to apply to every conversation, as they are not about the conversation itself, but how to psych yourself up to talk to people, and how to handle rejection without letting it ruin you.

Tip Seven- Get Out of Your Head

You have to get out of your own head to ever hold a good conversation with someone because you have to be able to approach someone to talk to them. If you are stuck in your head, and the "Oh I can't" thoughts, then you will be stuck at only talking to people you have to.

By getting out of your head, you will feel confident enough to approach a person that you have never met before, and that has no correlation to any of your friends. This is the best feeling, knowing that you can make friends anywhere, and not have to worry about going somewhere and not knowing anyone there.

Imagine you are going to a party. Your friend says that they will meet you there. You are glad, because you don't know anyone else who will be attending, or they are just minor acquaintances from work or school. You get there, and your friend texts you were saying that they can't come because something came up. You don't panic because you decide just to go find someone to talk to. You walk up to a guy or girl you have never seen before and strike up a conversation. Before the night is up, you have met seven new people that you really get along with.

That is what can happen once you stop the thoughts that you aren't good enough to talk to someone, or that you are too boring for anyone to want to talk to. Confidence is key. Boost yourself up, and as they say, fake it till you make it. You have to boost yourself up because there is not going to be anyone in the world who is able to make you feel better about yourself than you can. Go in with the mindset that you are worth talking to, and that you are funny and witty. By believing in yourself, people will be more open to you, as they can see that you are confident in yourself.

Tip Eight- Boost Your Self Esteem

This one goes hand in hand with getting out of your head. You have to believe in yourself to get out of your head. If you have low self-esteem, you will be more prone to rejection, because just like lions, people can pick out the ugly ones. No one wants to have to carry the entire conversation, so they generally steer away from the shy people, and gravitate to someone who they know will actively engage in conversation.

The way to boost your self-esteem can also involve a mirror. Stand in front of it for ten minutes a day only saying positive things about yourself. You are smart; you are strong, you are caring, you are kind. Do not mention any of your negative attributes. For every negative thing you say, add another minute to the time you spend looking in the mirror. It is your responsibility to build yourself up, no one else's. You can do it. As the days go on, you will find you are having to add less time onto your ten minutes, until finally, you spend just the ten minutes saying entirely positive things about yourself. Eventually, you will begin to believe them. You are essentially retraining your brain to say nice things to you, rather than mean things.

This society is so bleak, and some so many mean people say hateful things while hiding behind a computer screen, and this has cause self-esteem rates to go way down. Build yourself back up to stay above the hatred

Tip Nine- Handle Rejection with Pride

If you have low self-esteem, this will be hard, so you have to build yourself up to be able to do this. Otherwise, it will get to you, and make you not want to talk to people any longer. If you are rejected before you build yourself up, just take some time to recuperate.

Not everyone will want to talk to you, especially nowadays.

In today's age, people judge others before they even open their mouths, and decide on if a person is "worthy" of speaking to them. You have to break away from this thinking. You also cannot think that someone is above your level, they may seem like they are, and turn out to be the nicest person ever. However, when you approach someone, they may reject you, and this is okay. You may not want to talk to anyone that approaches you either.

If you are rejected, shake it off. Remind yourself that it is not you, it is who they are. They decided that they did not want to get to know you, and that is their loss, not yours. Get back up on that metaphorical horse and try again with someone else. You will find someone who is actually worth talking to.

Tip Ten- Don't Latch On

In a setting with a lot of people, it is so easy to try to find people that you enjoy talking to and staying with them a majority of the time. This is not a superb idea. You have to work for the crowd so to speak. How boring would it be if you were at a concert, and the singer only interacted with one fan? It is the same concept with talking to people. Go around to different people, and try to make more than one new friend. Eventually, you can come back to that one person, but let them have some time to talk to others, and give yourself time to talk to others as well.

How These Tips Help

These tips are for your own personal use to adapt to specific conversations and situation, and to psych yourself up before you go to a social event where you may not know someone that is there.

Following these tips will give you an edge on your conversations. Using these will help give you a self-esteem boost, and you will learn how to help yourself. These tips will make you a better conversationalist and a better you.

Chapter 6

After the Tips

If you have tried all of these tips, and find that you still cannot connect with people, you should try to see about getting some help with a psychiatrist. There could be some real deep-seated issues there. Talking to people is hard, but if you have tried to break out of your shell, and find yourself having panic attacks every time, you need to know what is going wrong.

There is nothing wrong with getting help either. Just as you would need to see a doctor for a physical illness, you should see a psychiatrist if your social anxiety is so bad that it is causing you to break down at the thought of talking to someone you do not know. There are a lot of resources that are at your disposal. If you are not sure a psychiatrist in your area, try talking to your average doctor, and he can help refer you to someone. The best thing about that is he is more likely to know a specialist to ensure that you are getting the best level of help that you can get.

How to know if it is more than just being shy

- You have panic attacks regularly in social situations: This can be the sign of a serious problem. You should get it checked out, and maybe the doctor can help you figure out how to work through it in a way that is best suited to you.

- You avoid stores during busy hours: If you would rather go without a necessity for a period of time because you do not want to visit a store during working hours as there will be too many people there, and could cause you to have a meltdown, you should see a doctor. This is serious. You cannot deny your needs. A physician can help you figure out the root of the problem, and set you on your way to healing.

- If you feel physically ill in social situations where there are only a handful of people: If being in small groups makes you feel physically ill, you should definitely look into it. Doing so allows you to truly live your life to the fullest, once you figure out what is wrong.

Don't let anxiety control your life any longer. Get the help you deserve and do not feel bad for doing so. You deserve to live a happy life unrestrained by anxiety. Regain control of your life.

Conclusion

Thank for making it through to the end of *The No. 1 Way to Prospect*, let's hope it was informative and able to provide you with all of the tools you need to achieve your goals whatever it may be.

The next step is to find the method of prospecting that works for you and begin to use it. In this book, you learned things that are going to help you to be more successful when you are prospecting and some of the things that you should stay away from but you may find work for you.

Not every technique is going to work for the same company, you have to do what is going to be best for your company, and if cold calling prospecting is going to be the best way to do that, then that is going to be the way for you. However, you need to keep in mind that many people are going to already know about your company and are going to buy the product if it meets their needs or if it has been recommended to them by someone else.

No matter what you are trying to sell, you are going to reach out to your prospects to make them customers. And hopefully, you are successful in your efforts!

Thank you and good luck!

THANK YOU

Dear treasured reader, I would like to thank you from the bottom of my heart for choosing to purchase this book. I hope you've gotten some valuable information that you can use right now to build a successful online business for yourself.

In case you missed it earlier, if you would like to receive latest tips and tricks on internet marketing, exclusive strategies, upcoming books & promotions, and **more,** do subscribe to my mailing list in the link below! I will be giving away a free book that you can download *right away* as well after you subscribe to show my appreciation!

Once again thank you and all the best to your success!
Jonathan S. Walker

About The Author

Hi there it's Jonathan Walker here, I want to share a little bit about myself so that we can get to know each other on a deeper level. I grew up in California, USA, and have lived there for the better part of my life. Being exposed to many different people and opportunities when I was young, it made me want to strive to become an entrepreneur to escape the rat race path that most of my peers had taken. I knew I wanted to be able to travel and experience the world the way it was meant to be seen and I've done just that. I've travelled to most places around the world and I'm enjoying every minute of it for sure. In my free time I love to play tennis and believe it or not, compose songs. I wish you all the best again in your endeavours, and may your dreams, whatever they may be, come true abundantly in the near future.

www.ingramcontent.com/pod-product-compliance
Lightning Source LLC
LaVergne TN
LVHW010346070526
838199LV00065B/5798